Choosing
to
Change

**A Client-Centred Approach to Alcohol
and Medication Use by Older Adults**

Centre
for Addiction and
Mental Health
Centre de
toxicomanie et
de santé mentale

The Addiction Research Foundation is a Division
of the Centre for Addiction and Mental Health

For information on other Addiction Research Foundation (ARF)
Division products, or to place an order, contact:

Centre for Addiction and Mental Health
Marketing Services
33 Russell Street
Toronto, ON M5S 2S1
Phone: 1-800-661-1111 or (416) 595-6059 in Toronto
E-mail: mktg@arf.org

Disponible en français   ISBN 0-88868-309-X

2030/06-98/1,500   PG096   Printed in Canada

The Wind, the Sun and the Traveller

One day, the wind and sun looked down and saw a traveller walking along a road. The wind bet the sun that the wind could force the traveller to remove his cloak. The wind blew and blew and blew some more. All that happened was that the traveller held to his cloak more tightly with every step. At last, the wind gave up. Now, it was the sun's turn. As the sun warmed the earth, the traveller felt warmer and warmer. First, he removed his scarf. The sun warmed the earth a little bit more. The traveller removed his hat. The sun warmed a bit more. And the traveller finally removed his cloak.

— based on an Aesop's Fable

Goals can be achieved through positive choices and a gradual approach to change.

Project Team

Jennifer Barr, Project Leader, Addiction Research Foundation,*
  Peterborough
Penny Stuart, Writer, Ottawa

ॐ

Jane Baron, Past Manager, Lifestyle Enrichment
  for Senior Adults (LESA), Ottawa
Christine Bois, Addiction Research Foundation,* Perth
Virginia Carver, Interim Project Leader, Addiction Research
  Foundation,* Ottawa
Margaret Flower, Metro Addiction Assessment Referral
  Service (MAARS), Toronto**
Wendy Freeman, Addiction Research Foundation,* Toronto
Simon Guillemette, Addiction Research Foundation,* Ottawa
Susan Harrison, Interim Project Leader, Addiction Research
  Foundation,* East Region
Margaret Kittel Canale, Addiction Research Foundation,* Toronto
Lise Nolet, Addiction Research Foundation,* Toronto
Lorna Sagorsky, Addiction Research Foundation,* Toronto
Cindy Smythe, Addiction Research Foundation,* London
Elizabeth Turnbull, Addiction Research Foundation,* Toronto

EDITING & TRANSLATION
Julia Drake, Drake Communications, Toronto
Myles Magner, Addiction Research Foundation,* Toronto
Élise Parent, Addiction Research Foundation,* Toronto

GRAPHIC DESIGN
Paula Poschun, Addiction Research Foundation,* Toronto

* The Addiction Research Foundation is a Division of the Centre for Addiction
  and Mental Health.

** MAARS is a program of the Donwood Institute, a Division of the
  Centre for Addiction and Mental Health.

Acknowledgments

The project team gratefully acknowledges the contributions and support of the following individuals and organizations, without which the development of *Choosing to Change* would not have been possible.

RESEARCH

The ideas and materials in this handbook have been developed from evaluations of the Lifestyle Enrichment for Senior Adults (LESA) program at the Centretown Community Health Centre in Ottawa and the Community Older Persons Alcohol (COPA) Program in Toronto. Thank you to those clients, volunteers and counsellors who shared their experiences.

The recent report entitled *Participatory Research on Innovative Addictions Treatment for Older Adults: Clients of the LESA Program Describe What Makes a Difference*, by Paulette West and Kathryn Graham, made a significant contribution to the content of this handbook.

NEEDS ASSESSMENT

Early steps that were taken to provide the direction for the ultimate development of this handbook began with a needs assessment of service providers in the province of Ontario. We thank the survey respondents who willingly shared their views, and Helen Youngson for the needs assessment and report.

FOCUS GROUPS

A second step involved focus groups in which individuals from the field provided open and articulate expression of their needs.

We are grateful to the participants, to the team members who lent assistance to the process, and to Maryanne Hicks for the co-ordination and the report.

PILOT SITES

Access Centre for Community Care in Lanark, Leeds and
  Grenville, Brockville
The Metropolitan Toronto Housing Company Limited, Toronto
Psychiatric Assessment Services, Peterborough Civic Hospital,
  Peterborough
Service de Santé d'Ottawa-Carleton/Ottawa-Carleton Health
  Department, Ottawa
Warden Woods Community Centre, Toronto

REVIEWERS

Thank you to the following people who reviewed various drafts
of the handbook and contributed to its content:
Kathryn Graham, Addiction Research Foundation,* London
Pearl Isaac, Addiction Research Foundation,* Toronto
Wendy Knowles, Psychiatric Assessment Service for the Elderly,
  Peterborough
Christine McKay, Lifestyle Enrichment for Senior Adults, Ottawa
Eileen McKee, Community Older Persons Alcohol Program,
  Toronto
Philip Moorman, Lifestyle Enrichment for Senior Adults, Ottawa
Michele Morin, Lifestyle Enrichment for Senior Adults, Ottawa
Patrick Smith, Addiction Research Foundation,* Toronto

* The Addiction Research Foundation is a Division of the Centre for Addiction
  and Mental Health.

SPECIAL ACKNOWLEDGMENTS

Special credit is acknowledged for the time and collaboration of Margaret Flower and the support of her agency, Metro Addiction Assessment Referral Service (MAARS).**

The project team would like to especially thank Jane Baron. Since her retirement, she has shared her experience and wisdom, and given many days of her time to this project. She contributed substantially to many of the approaches incorporated in this handbook.

** MAARS is a program of the Donwood Institute, a Division of the Centre for Addiction and Mental Health.

Contents

Introduction

This handbook is for professional staff of health and social service agencies who, in their work with older adults, encounter people with problems associated with alcohol and psychoactive medications. People working in addiction treatment programs who are developing or expanding services for older adults may also find this handbook useful.

The approach taken in this handbook is holistic and client-centred, and it accepts that harm reduction, or reduced substance use (as compared with abstinence), may be an acceptable treatment goal. This approach to working with clients with substance use problems may differ from the approaches you have used in the past.

This handbook stresses that substance use problems are best addressed within the overall context of helping older adults to improve their general health and well-being. You can play an important role in helping older adults make lifestyle changes that will improve their overall health *and* reduce or eliminate problems with substance use.

As a professional caregiver, you have a unique advantage in assisting clients. You have many of the communication and support skills that are necessary in helping to reduce or alleviate problems with alcohol or psychoactive medications.

This handbook is designed to help you understand the dynamics around substance use and allow you to feel more comfortable when talking with clients about the issue.

The handbook is organized into seven sections, with appendices, as follows:

SECTION 1: BACKGROUND

Section 1 provides background on why different treatment options are needed for older adults. It also describes two Canadian programs that have been successful in working with older adults who have problems associated with their use of alcohol and medication. Both programs have a flexible client-centred approach.

SECTION 2: THE CLIENT — IDENTIFYING THE PROBLEM

Section 2 looks at the client, low-risk drinking guidelines, problem use, as well as some of the difficulties in distinguishing alcohol and/or medication problems from changes often associated with aging. It also points out ways in which older clients differ from other age groups in their reasons for using alcohol or medication as well as the effects and patterns of use.

SECTION 3: THINGS TO KNOW ABOUT ALCOHOL AND MEDICATION USE

Section 3 provides additional information on alcohol and medication, including various interactions that can occur if alcohol is combined with common medications. This section also examines withdrawal from various psychoactive substances.

SECTION 4: ASSESSMENT AND STAGES OF CHANGE

Section 4 examines some issues in the assessment process with older adults and reviews what is known as the "stages of change model" and its application to substance use problems.

SECTION 5: HOW TO HELP

Section 5 examines ways to help older adults with substance use problems. It emphasizes the importance of building a relationship with the client as a precursor to addressing substance use issues.

SECTION 6: COMMON QUESTIONS

Section 6 poses and answers common questions that come up when helping a person with problems related to alcohol or medication.

SECTION 7: CLIENT PROFILES

Section 7 describes two typical clients and illustrates the process of intervening with an older adult with a substance use problem.

APPENDICES

Appendix A lists further sources of information.
Appendix B provides a monitoring form that could help clients keep track of their drinking.

REFERENCES

The References section lists materials used as background information in developing this handbook.

Glossary

Counsellors include health and social service professionals, with the various titles of clinician, therapist and service provider, who see older adults in their work or their practices.

Denial is the tendency of people to minimize or deny the amount and/or effect of alcohol or medication in their lives. Denial is sometimes viewed as a barrier in the treatment of problems with alcohol and medication use.

Drug is a term used for a substance "whenever its use is intended primarily to bring about change in some existing process or state, be it psychological, physiological or biochemical" (Jacobs & Fehr, 1987). In the context of this handbook, the term "drug" generally refers to psychoactive drugs. This includes alcohol, which is a central nervous system depressant drug, and medication as well as other drugs.

Harm Reduction is an approach that focuses on reducing the risks and harm associated with substance use. Programs using a harm reduction approach work with the client to achieve practical short-term improvements in health and to reduce the harm associated with substance use to both the user and society. Early public health examples of a harm reduction approach include needle exchange programs and methadone maintenance programs. Specialized programs for older adults with substance use problems also employ a harm reduction approach.

Medications are either non-prescription or prescribed drugs that can be obtained from a store or pharmacy. In the context of this handbook, the term "medications" refers to mood-altering or psychoactive medications that may cause problems for older adults. These are generally central nervous system depressant medications such as sleeping pills or tranquillizers and pain medications, including those containing codeine or hydrocodone.

Older Adults are generally defined as people aged 65 years and older. In some cases, people in the 55- to 64-year-old category will need the specialized approach outlined in the handbook, because their life circumstances are similar to many older adults (e.g., they may no longer be working, they may experience poor physical health or social isolation).

Physical Dependence occurs when a person's body adapts to the presence of a drug, develops tolerance to its effects and experiences withdrawal symptoms if he or she stops using the drug.

Psychoactive Drugs are drugs that interact with the central nervous system to produce changes in feeling, mood or perception, and in orientation to self and the environment. They are sometimes called mind-altering or mood-altering drugs.

Psychological Dependence occurs when using a given drug becomes so central to a person's thoughts, emotions and activities that he or she finds it extremely difficult to stop using the drug.

Relapse is a return to problematic levels of substance use after a period of abstinence or reduced use. A relapse may be a brief episode (often called a lapse) or a more prolonged episode of substance use.

Substance is a term used in the addictions field to refer to drugs (including alcohol) that can produce physical and/or psychological dependence.

Tolerance occurs when the body has adapted to a drug and loses some sensitivity to its effects. A person who has developed tolerance to a drug requires an increased amount or more frequent use of the drug to experience the original effect.

Section 1

Background

- A Client-Centred Approach

- Why Different Treatment Options Are Needed

- Successful Counselling Relationships

While Pauline was working, she kept her drinking under control. She took her work seriously, so she never drank during the week. After retirement, she moved in with her sister, Laura, to share expenses. Then, she started to drink every day. Laura stopped entertaining, because she never knew how intoxicated Pauline would be when guests arrived. Laura was particularly upset that Pauline smoked in bed. Pauline thought that her sister was overreacting because Laura opposed smoking and alcohol on moral grounds. When Pauline fell and broke her hip, Laura ended up caring for her. Although they pretended that it was an accident, they both knew alcohol was a factor in the fall.

After counselling, Pauline continued to drink heavily. However, as in her days in the workforce, she set some limits. She never drank before 5 p.m. She went out when her sister was entertaining. She made a rule never to smoke in the bedroom. She paid to clean the drapes and carpets. The two sisters made peace and started cooking together and sharing meals again.

A Client-Centred Approach

This may not seem like the most desirable outcome. In the best of all worlds, Pauline might stop drinking and smoking entirely. Sometimes, however, the counsellor's goal will be to help a person make small changes that will benefit his or her overall health and safety. As the person's life and relationships improve, bigger changes may follow. In other situations, if clients are ready, counsellors may work with them toward goals of low-risk drinking or abstinence.

This handbook describes an approach to counselling and working with older adults with substance use problems that helps clients to make changes. The approach is flexible, and it supports people as they make choices for themselves. The approach also respects each individual's preferred pace for making changes. Sometimes, this involves accepting decisions that the counsellor may not feel are in the client's best interests. Sometimes, this involves accepting that small steps may be the only steps that a client is ready and able to take.

The approach takes its inspiration from two Canadian programs that pioneered client-centred treatment for older adults with problems related to substance use. The Lifestyle Enrichment for Senior Adults (LESA) program began in 1981 at the Centretown Community Health Centre, a neighborhood-based health and social service agency in downtown Ottawa. The Community Older Persons Alcohol (COPA) Program was established in west Toronto in 1983.

The approach used by both programs is non-confrontational, holistic, nurturing and respectful of the individual's desires and capabilities. The programs use a combination of individual counselling (often in the client's home), group support and recreational activity. They were developed specifically to meet the needs of hard-to-reach older adults.

LESA and COPA were developed during a time — the 1980s — when many addiction treatment programs viewed problematic substance use as a disease, with abstinence as the major goal of treatment. At the time, many believed that other life changes could only be made after abstinence had been achieved.

LESA and COPA counsellors approach clients differently than do other counsellors. LESA and COPA counsellors do not ask people to acknowledge problems with alcohol or medication use or to embrace abstinence in order to receive help. Instead, they help older clients deal with problems with alcohol and medication use as part of addressing a range of life and health issues. They help clients to understand the effects of alcohol and medications on their health, and they support clients to develop the means to reduce or eliminate problematic use.

This handbook brings together the approaches that work best for LESA and COPA counsellors. Examples used throughout the handbook have been changed to protect client confidentiality.

Why Different Treatment Options Are Needed

Many addiction treatment programs, while beneficial for younger clients, may not have the specialized program elements to address the life issues, medical problems and medication use of older adults. A 65-year-old man experiencing problems related to medication use may not have much in common with a 25-year-old man with a cocaine problem. A 70-year-old widow who has a recent history of drinking has different needs from those of a 40-year-old business owner with a chronic alcohol problem. Thus, different treatment options are needed for older adults for some of the following reasons:

• Issues relevant to the lives of younger adults (e.g., jobs, marriage, raising children, involvement with the legal system) may not be relevant to the lives of older clients.

• Issues relevant to the lives of older adults (e.g., age-related health problems, loss of loved ones and other losses, changes in roles, isolation) may not be relevant to the lives of younger adults.

• Some older adults may be reluctant or unable to leave their homes to attend a treatment program. Also, some treatment programs may not be accessible to older clients. For example, programs may not be close to public transport, may not have elevators or wheelchair access, or may not provide program materials that can be easily read by older adults.

• Many addiction programs focus on abstinence or reduced drinking as a major goal of treatment. Some older adults may be reluctant to enter a program where abstinence or reduced drinking is a required goal or where participants are asked to acknowledge a problem with substance use as a criterion for participating. For some older adults, the stigma of attending an addiction treatment program may be a major deterrent to seeking help.

• Some addiction treatment programs geared for younger adults are too tiring for older adults in terms of the length of individual or group counselling sessions, the attendance requirements or the required activities. An approach that addresses older adults' pace and individual needs, and that is respectful of their individual experiences, may have a better chance of helping older adults to reach their goals than would a more structured treatment program.

Successful Counselling Relationships

The Lifestyle Enrichment for Senior Adults (LESA) program in Ottawa found that counsellors' attitudes were associated with success in building a positive relationship with older clients (Bergin & Baron, 1992). Successful counsellors had the following qualities:

They were:
- comfortable working with clients who had problems with alcohol and/or medication use
- able to accept each client's pace, seeing value in small changes
- genuinely respectful and accepting of clients
- realistically encouraging and supportive of clients
- more process-oriented than results-oriented
- clear and consistent about desired counselling outcomes, yet flexible in the use of counselling techniques
- creative in finding ways to motivate clients
- able to let clients advocate for themselves, doing it for them only when necessary
- oriented toward holistic health
- positive and optimistic, yet accepting of the inevitability of death
- capable of working in a multi-disciplinary community setting
- of the belief that older adults are capable of change and growth.

In their feedback about the LESA program, what clients valued most overall was the ability to set their own pace and the lack of pressure.

Section 2

The Client — Identifying the Problem

- Who Is the Client?

- Older Adults' Use of Alcohol and Medication

- When Does Substance Use Become a Problem?

- Low-Risk Drinking Guidelines

- Distinguishing Problems with Alcohol
  and Medication from Symptoms Associated
  with Age-related Illness

- Reasons for Alcohol and/or Medication Use

- Life Patterns of Substance Use

- Summary

Pete, 75, sits alone in his apartment, drinking a beer and waiting for his home-care worker to arrive. He is happy that she is coming, because he'd like to talk to someone. He's having problems again with his landlord. And his hip is worse — he can barely walk. Then, he remembers that his home-care worker might ask about his medication. He can't remember if he took his pill today or not. He goes to the cupboard and takes two pills just to be sure. One green. One red. Pete finishes his beer and carefully puts the bottle away. No need for her to know that it's his fourth drink of the day.

Grace, 67, was never interested in drinking. She was always too busy raising three children and running a busy household. There was the odd weekend binge, but nothing serious. Then, two years ago, her husband died. All their plans for retirement died with him. Their lives were so intertwined. Last year, her sister died after a long, painful time with cancer. At first, Grace just took a drink or two at night to help her sleep. The sleeping problems worsened. Now, she is drinking every night and sometimes earlier in the day. Once immaculately groomed, Grace isn't taking care of herself anymore. Old friends are avoiding her. Her grandchildren suspect that she's getting senile, but they have their own lives. Besides, she's not hurting anyone, they conclude.

❧

Who Is the Client?

Counsellors who work with older adults probably meet people like Pete and Grace many times in the course of their work. Sometimes, as is the case with Grace, problems with alcohol are recent and linked to specific life events. Sometimes, as in Pete's case, the history of problems with substance use is long or hidden, and the person is dealing with a range of health problems, including problems related to both alcohol and psychoactive medication use.

Who is the client? Clearly, older adults are a heterogeneous group. Those who enjoy stable health, adequate finances and good relationships are worlds apart from those struggling with major illness, poverty or grieving recent losses. Heredity, lifestyle, diet, attitudes, spiritual beliefs and life experiences influence the way people age and the way they look at life and at themselves.

Nevertheless, there are similarities in the patterns of alcohol and medication use among older adults — patterns that are distinct from those of younger age groups.

Older Adults' Use of Alcohol and Medication

Listed below are a few facts about older adults' use of alcohol and non-prescription or prescribed medications.

ALCOHOL
• In general, older adults who do drink consume less alcohol than do younger adults.

• Small amounts of alcohol can worsen some health conditions — such as diabetes, heart or blood pressure problems, liver disease or stomach problems — that are more common in older adults.

• Alcohol is a depressant which acts on the central nervous system and reduces alertness, co-ordination, judgment and reaction time, and increases the risk of falls or accidents. The consequences of falls or accidents can be more severe for older adults.

• Psychoactive medications (e.g., sleeping pills and tranquillizers) are prescribed more often to older adults than younger adults. Alcohol may increase the effect or adversely interact with these medications.

• Older adults are generally more sensitive to the effects of alcohol. This is because their blood circulation, kidneys and liver work more slowly to eliminate alcohol, and their bodies contain less water to dilute alcohol. Women are generally smaller than men and have proportionally less water in their bodies to dilute alcohol, so older women are even more sensitive to alcohol's effects.

MEDICATION

• Older adults are rarely involved with illegal drugs. Compared with younger age groups, however, older adults are prescribed more medication, including psychoactive drugs, and they are higher users of non-prescription medicines.

• Older adults are more likely than younger adults to use multiple prescribed and non-prescription medications at the same time, often to treat chronic physical illnesses.

• Older adults may experience problems stemming from long-term use of psychoactive medication that was prescribed when such drugs were given out more freely than today.

• Older adults are generally more sensitive than younger adults to the effects of medication. This is because their blood circulation, kidneys and liver work more slowly to eliminate medication, and their bodies contain less water to dilute medication. Women are generally smaller than men and have proportionally less water in their bodies to dilute medication, so older women are even more sensitive to the effects of medication.

When Does Substance Use Become a Problem?

It is most useful to think about problems with substance use as being on a continuum. The earlier that you can intervene in the development of problems, the greater the likelihood that the client will be able to make the necessary life changes. Problem use of alcohol or psychoactive medications can affect many systems of the body, as well as many other aspects of a person's well-being — psychosocial (e.g., relationships, memory), spiritual and environmental (e.g., living conditions in the home).

Although the risk of a person developing problems increases with a higher volume and/or frequency of substance use, problems can and do occur at very low levels of use (e.g., a few drinks a day, combined with a psychoactive medication). For some clients, the effects of substance use will be very visible and easily identified (e.g., they have a long history of heavy drinking, which has resulted in multiple physical and psychosocial problems). For others, it may be difficult to determine whether their use of substances is contributing to the difficulties they are experiencing (e.g., they may be combining a therapeutic dosage of psychoactive medication such as a tranquillizer with one or two drinks during the evening and experience some confusion, dizziness or falls).

Here is a simple definition of **problem substance use**: A problem exists when the use of a substance(s) results in negative consequences for the person, and the person continues to use the substance(s) despite these negative consequences. Negative consequences may affect physical health, environment, relationships, spirituality, legal status or other areas of the person's life.

Low-Risk Drinking Guidelines

Some people experience negative consequences from drinking because they are simply unaware of low-risk drinking levels. Others have not adjusted their drinking to account for the body's decreased ability to handle alcohol as they age. Older adults are more vulnerable than other adults to the effects of even small amounts of alcohol, the combination of alcohol and medication, or multiple medications. Women of all ages are more vulnerable than men to the effects of alcohol and medication. (For more information on women and substance use, see *The Hidden Majority: A Guidebook on Alcohol and Other Drug Issues for Counsellors Who Work with Women.*)

The guidelines below should be shared with clients since they provide some goals to work toward in reducing harmful drinking levels. However, it is important to note that these guidelines may be too high for many older adults and people who have had problems with alcohol.

Guidelines for low-risk drinking for healthy adults endorsed
by the Addiction Research Foundation and the Ontario Public
Health Association in 1997 include the following:

• Drink no more than two standard drinks on any day.
• Limit weekly intake to 14 or fewer standard drinks
  for men and nine or fewer standard drinks for women.
• Drink slowly to avoid intoxication, waiting at least
  one hour between drinks and taking alcohol with food
  and non-alcoholic beverages.
• If you abstain, don't start drinking alcohol for its protective
  effect against heart disease; less risky alternatives include
  exercise, better nutrition and quitting smoking.
• If you choose to drink, the protective effects of alcohol
  can be achieved with as little as one drink every other day.
• If you are seeking help for a drinking problem, follow
  the advice of your counsellor or health professional.

A standard drink is defined as 341 mL (12 oz.) of beer (5 per cent
alcohol); 142 mL (5 oz.) of table wine (12 per cent alcohol);
43 mL (1.5 oz.) of liquor (40 per cent alcohol); or 85 mL (3 oz.)
of fortified wine, such as sherry or port (18 per cent alcohol).

A "STANDARD DRINK" =

Beer		Table Wine		Liquor		Fortified Wine
341 mL	**or**	142 mL	**or**	43 mL	**or**	85 mL
(12 oz.)		(5 oz.)		(1.5 oz.)		(3 oz.)

Distinguishing Problems with Alcohol and Medication from Symptoms Associated with Age-related Illness

Identifying problems with alcohol or medication in older adults can be difficult, because symptoms sometimes resemble the changes associated with age-related illnesses. Symptoms that could indicate a substance use problem in a younger person are sometimes attributed to aging in an older adult. Is falling down a sign of intoxication, a sign of problematic use of medication, or a sign of unsteadiness related to decreased mobility or a bone disease? Is forgetfulness a sign of depression, a sign of dementia, a sign of alcohol use, or a long-standing characteristic of a person who now happens to be old?

The following table (ARF, 1993) illustrates how the signs of alcohol and medication use can sometimes be mistaken as signs of aging (and vice versa):

TABLE 1: Comparing Signs of Alcohol and/or Medication Use with Signs of Aging

Possible Signs of Alcohol and/or Medication Use	Signs of Aging*
Confusion	Confusion
Disorientation	Disorientation
Recent memory loss	Recent memory loss
Slowed thought process	Slowed thought process
Loss of muscle co-ordination and loss of balance	Loss of muscle co-ordination and loss of balance
Tremors	Tremors
Gastritis	Gastritis
Depression	Depression
Irregular heartbeat	Irregular heart beat
High blood pressure	High blood pressure
Malnutrition (poor nutrition), dehydration	Malnutrition (poor nutrition), dehydration

* Although these signs are associated with aging, they should not be construed as inevitable consequences of the aging process.

Reasons for Alcohol and/or Medication Use

Clinicians report that, when older adults experience problems with substance use, the reasons for use often differ from those of younger people. Older adults may experience a variety of life issues that can increase their risk of problems with alcohol or medication. These can include stresses related to the following areas:

• Psychosocial — retirement; changing roles in the family; loss of companionship through death of a partner, close friends, family

members or pets; decreased mobility; loss of memory; boredom; sadness; anxiety; depression and trauma, including physical or sexual abuse or war experiences
• Spiritual — unresolved grief; mourning over loss of health; losing hope; and coming to terms with death
• Physical — lack of energy; physical aches and pain; and sleep disturbances
• Environmental — financial difficulties; housing problems; loss of independence; lack of support services; and "ageism" (i.e., lack of respect shown for older adults in the community and society).

In addition, an older adult may continue to use a substance hazardously because he or she has become dependent on the substance and feels unable to stop.

Life Patterns of Substance Use

Older adults' problems with alcohol and/or psychoactive medications can generally be divided into three groups with distinct profiles and challenges: early onset, intermittent and late onset.

EARLY ONSET
• *Early onset* refers to problems with alcohol or psychoactive medication that a person first experiences early in life and which continue over time. Typically, counsellors report that people with early onset problems come to treatment between 50 and 60 years of age, although these clients may have been involved with the treatment system over the years.

People with early onset problems include those who are often referred to as "chronic alcoholics." Characteristically, they have tried to stop using many times. However, they may feel overwhelmed by current problems and hopeless about the future. They may lack confidence in their ability to change and see the odds as stacked against them. In addition, based on previous experiences during withdrawal, they may fear they will die the next time they try to quit.

• The *challenge* with people who have early onset problems is often to help build successes and hopefulness into a life where the consequences of years of substance use problems have taken a significant toll.

The negative consequences that are associated with long-term substance use may need attention. For example, the client may require better housing, improved nutrition, adequate medical attention or help in organizing finances. For a counsellor, it can be a challenge to stay hopeful and resourceful when there are serious chronic issues.

INTERMITTENT
• *Intermittent* refers to problems with alcohol or psychoactive medication that a person experiences in episodes throughout his or her life, often separated by long periods without problem use. Typically, clients with intermittent problems seek treatment because of a crisis in their lives.

Generally, those with intermittent problems have been able to control their psychoactive medication and alcohol use. On occasion, however, family problems, legal problems or work-related stresses would result in increased use and subsequent problems related to that use. When each episode or problem ended, the problematic use of alcohol and/or medications would usually end as well.

• The *challenge* is to help people with intermittent problems recognize that physical sensitivity to alcohol and medication increases with age and that the risk associated with periodic heavy substance use also increases with age.

• Other *challenges* with intermittent problems (which are also challenges with late onset problems) include identifying and addressing the underlying issues that have prompted change in the client's former pattern of use, and finding ways to educate the client about the effects of alcohol and/or psychoactive medication use.

Intermittent users may see no relationship between their substance use and their current problems. They may state correctly that they use the same amount or less medication and/or alcohol than they once did. For a counsellor, the intermittent nature of problems can make identification and treatment difficult (see also *Late Onset*).

LATE ONSET
• *Late onset* refers to problems with alcohol or psychoactive medication that a person first experiences late in life. Typically, counsellors say that late onset problems begin after age 65.

In younger years, people with late onset characteristics may have used psychoactive medications periodically or alcohol socially, but they did not experience problems related to that use. Alcohol or psychoactive medication problems developed in their senior years as a result of increased levels of consumption and/or increased sensitivity to these substances. Generally, they can recall clearly why they began to increase their substance use.

Their reasons are often age-related (i.e., changes in lifestyle following retirement or losses associated with aging). At the point of seeking help, most have suffered fewer physical, emotional or financial losses than people with early onset problems. Thus, their habits are not well entrenched. Their support systems are likely to be intact.

• The *challenges* with late onset problems (which are also challenges with intermittent problems) include identifying and addressing the underlying issues that have prompted change in the client's former pattern of use, and finding ways to educate the client about the effects of alcohol and/or psychoactive medication use.

Often, the cause of the change in substance use is easily recognized. The personal history of the late onset client will often show a fairly recent loss, change in role or change in health status. It is important to listen to the client's feelings about recent changes in his or her life over the past few years (i.e., the past five years) and how he or she is dealing with those changes. Is the client, for example, dealing with unresolved grief issues by drinking or taking psychoactive medication?

Clinicians have found that people with late onset characteristics are generally most receptive to lifestyle change directed to problem resolution. While they may not initially recognize their problems as being related to substance use, they have recent memories of feeling better and operating at a higher level. They often have higher self-esteem and self-confidence than users whose problem use began earlier in life. For the counsellor, the *dual challenge* is to address the crisis that triggered the change and to help the client understand the harmful effects of alcohol and/or medication use.

Summary

Compared with younger adults, older adults generally consume less alcohol, but they are more likely to use psychoactive medication. Older adults are generally more vulnerable than younger adults to the effects of psychoactive substances. Problem use exists on a continuum, and problems can occur at quite low levels of use in older adults. For this reason, it is important for older adults to be aware of low-risk drinking guidelines. Problems associated with alcohol and psychoactive medication use may be mistaken for signs of aging. Older adults who experience problems with alcohol or psychoactive medication fall into three groups: early onset, intermittent and late onset.

Section 3

Things to Know about Alcohol and Medication Use

- Chronic Diseases and Alcohol

- Alcohol and Medication Interactions

- Dependence and Withdrawal

- Summary

Chronic Diseases and Alcohol

Some older adults have chronic medical conditions that may interfere with their ability to metabolize medication or alcohol. Alcohol interferes with the control of many chronic diseases, including diabetes, epilepsy, gout, high blood pressure and heart problems.

Alcohol and Medication Interactions

Alcohol may interact with a medication. Alcohol's interactions with common medications are summarized in Table 2. The severity and significance of mixing alcohol and medication can be influenced by factors such as the following:
• age
• gender
• amount consumed
• whether drinking is chronic or occasional
• general health
• the combination of medications being used.

Remember these facts:
• Alcohol can mask important warning symptoms of disease (e.g., angina pain in cardiac patients).
• Organ damage due to alcohol may alter responses to medication.
• Combining alcohol with medication can compromise the effectiveness of the medication, which may aggravate the medical problems.
• Older adults tend to be more sensitive to the effects of both alcohol and medication, and they often use several medications at the same time.

TABLE 2: Some Interactions of Common Medications with Alcohol
NOTE: *In addition to the interactions listed below, many others are possible.*

Condition being treated	Some common medications (and examples of trade names)	Combined with alcohol can cause
Allergies, coughs, colds	Diphenhydramine (Benadryl®) Chlorpheniramine-containing medications (e.g., Chlor-Tripolon®, Contac C®, Neo Citran®) Other combinations (e.g., Triaminic®, Actifed®, Benylin® with codeine, Robitussin AC®)	Increased sleepiness Excessive drowsiness Impaired co-ordination Slurred speech Mental confusion Increased risk of falls Rapid intoxication Less common: Difficulty breathing Loss of consciousness Death *Possible reactions can range from mild (increased sleepiness) to severe (loss of consciousness and death).*
Anxiety, insomnia	*Benzodiazepines:* Diazepam (Novodipam®, Valium®) Chlordiazepoxide (Librium®) Lorazepam (Ativan®) Oxazepam (Serax®) Triazolam (Halcion®) Alprazolam (Xanax®) Temazepam (Restoril®) Clonazepam (Rivotril®)	

Condition being treated		Combined with alcohol can cause
Anxiety, insomnia (cont'd.)	Flurazepam (Dalmane®)	Increased sleepiness Excessive drowsiness Impaired co-ordination Slurred speech Mental confusion Increased risk of falls Rapid intoxication Less common: Difficulty breathing Loss of consciousness Death *Possible reactions can range from mild (increased sleepiness) to severe (loss of consciousness and death).*
Depression		
Epilepsy		
Gastro-intestinal disorders		
Hypertension		
Muscle spasms		

Condition being treated	Some common medications (and examples of trade names)	Combined with alcohol can cause
Nausea	*Sedative/Hypnotics:* Butalbital-containing medications (e.g., Fiorinal®); Chloral hydrate; Dimenhydrinate (e.g., Sleep Eeze®, Gravol®, Sominex®); Phenobarbital	Increased sleepiness; Excessive drowsiness; Impaired co-ordination; Slurred speech; Mental confusion; Increased risk of falls; Rapid intoxication. Less common: Difficulty breathing; Loss of consciousness; Death
Pain	Amitriptyline (Elavil®); Doxepin (Sinequan®); Imipramine (Tofranil®); Fluvoxamine (Luvox®); Trazodone (Desyrel®); Paroxetine (Paxil®)	
Psychoses	Phenobarbital; Phenytoin (Dilantin®); Primidone (Mysoline®); Carbamazepine (Tegretol®); Clonazepam (Rivotril®)	*Possible reactions can range from mild (increased sleepiness) to severe (loss of consciousness and death).*
Angina, hypertension	Metoclopramide (Maxeran®); Ranitidine (Zantac®); Verapamil (Isoptin®)	Dizziness, fainting, possible loss of consciousness
Blood-clotting disorders	Cyclobenzaprine (Flexeril®)	Increase in stomach irritation; may result in bleeding

Condition being treated		Combined with alcohol can cause
Pain (arthritis, inflammation or fever)	Methocarbamol (e.g., Robaxin®, Robaxisal®)	Increase in stomach irritation; may result in bleeding
Bacterial infections		Altered effect of antibiotics
Fungal infections		Possible serious disulfiram (Antabuse®) reaction (e.g., flushing, headache, weakness, nausea, vomiting, rapid heartbeat, shortness of breath)
Diabetes		
Arthritis or cancer		Increased risk of liver damage, especially with chronic alcohol use
Pain or fever		Increased risk of liver damage, especially with chronic alcohol use

Source: Addiction Research Foundation, Lifestyle Enrichment for Senior Adults and the Community Older Persons Alcohol Program (1993).

Dependence and Withdrawal

DEPENDENCE

People who use psychoactive substances on a regular basis may become dependent on them. People who are dependent on a given drug may experience physical dependence, psychological dependence and/or tolerance to the drug's effects.

• *Physical Dependence* occurs when a person's body adapts to the presence of a drug, develops tolerance to its effects and experiences withdrawal symptoms if he or she stops using the drug.

• *Psychological Dependence* occurs when using a given drug becomes so central to a person's thoughts, emotions and activities that he or she finds it extremely difficult to stop using the drug.

• *Tolerance* occurs when the body has adapted to a drug and loses some sensitivity to its effects. A person who has developed tolerance to a drug requires an increased amount or more frequent use of the drug to experience the original effect.

WITHDRAWAL

Clients who stop or reduce their use of psychoactive substances may experience withdrawal complications. For some people, withdrawal complications can be serious or life-threatening. Also, people who have a long history of using a substance can be very reluctant to stop or reduce their use because they are afraid of withdrawal. Such people may continue to drink, despite the fact that drinking has ceased to produce the desired effects and may be making them physically very ill.

For older clients, the problems of withdrawal can be compounded by other health or life issues. As a counsellor, one of your goals is to encourage clients to make healthy lifestyle choices. However, if a client decides to stop or reduce her or his use of drugs or alcohol, this should be done under the supervision of, or in consultation with, a physician or other knowledgeable health professional (e.g., at a detoxification centre). Psychoactive medications that have been used for a long time should always be tapered off, according to a schedule prescribed by a physician, rather than stopped suddenly.

NOTE: If you are concerned that the client may experience withdrawal complications, contact your nearest detoxification centre or a physician knowledgeable about substance use problems. (In Ontario, clinical advice is also available from the ARF Clinical Consultation Service at 1-838-720-ACCS.)

Alcohol Withdrawal*
• Psychological dependence can occur even for someone consuming relatively moderate amounts of alcohol, particularly if daily drinking has been part of the person's life. Withdrawal can bring anxiety and, sometimes, feelings of panic.

• Physical dependence occurs in consistently heavy drinkers. Sometimes it can be difficult to judge the extent of physical dependence, because many heavy drinkers have built up a high tolerance for alcohol and may not appear intoxicated.

Alcohol withdrawal can follow extended periods of heavy daily drinking. It begins six to 24 hours after a person's last drink, and

---

*Adapted from Kahan (1997).

may persist for up to seven days. Symptoms can include tremors, sweating, fast pulse, high blood pressure, vomiting and anxiety. Grand mal seizures are possible. Other later complications can include irregular heartbeat, hallucinations and delirium tremens (the DTs). Patients with delirium tremens become confused and disoriented, and may die of cardiovascular collapse. Therefore, people with a history of serious or complicated alcohol withdrawal symptoms such as seizures should be referred to a physician for assessment.

Alcohol withdrawal is effectively treated by providing a calm, supportive environment and (if necessary) careful use of benzodiazepines.

Benzodiazepine Withdrawal*
Benzodiazepine (e.g., alprazolam, chlordiazepoxide, diazepam, triazolam) withdrawal can include anxiety symptoms (e.g., emotional volatility, insomnia, irritability, poor concentration, panic attacks) and neurological symptoms (e.g., mild visual distortions, blurry vision, unsteadiness of gait).

Abrupt withdrawal from high doses of benzodiazepines used over time can cause complications such as seizures, confusion and hallucinations. Clients wishing to discontinue their benzodiazepine use should always consult with a physician.

Opioid (Narcotic) Withdrawal*
Opiate (e.g., codeine, hydrocodone, oxycodone) withdrawal symptoms are somewhat similar to a bad case of the flu. Symptoms include sweating, muscle aches, runny nose and

---

*Adapted from Kahan (1997).

runny eyes, goose bumps, chills and nausea. Clients in opiate withdrawal are restless and uncomfortable, and they experience cravings. Symptoms generally go away over several days and withdrawal is not fatal. On the other hand, an overdose of an opioid can be fatal.

Sedative/Hypnotic (Barbiturate) Withdrawal*

Clients who abruptly stop high doses of barbiturate-containing sedative/hypnotics (e.g., Fiorinal®, amobarbital, secobarbital) will experience withdrawal symptoms that may be fatal. Clients should always be referred for a medical assessment if withdrawing from high doses of these drugs. Since the development of safer medications for the treatment of anxiety and depression, barbiturates are prescribed much less frequently than in the past. Overdoses with these drugs are frequently fatal.

Summary

Many older clients use medication to treat health problems. Alcohol may interfere with the treatment of these problems. If a client plans to stop using a substance, it is important to determine the possibility of withdrawal complications and to seek appropriate support and treatment.

---

*Adapted from Kahan (1997).

Section 4

Assessment and Stages of Change

- Assessment

- Stages of Change Model

- Relapse

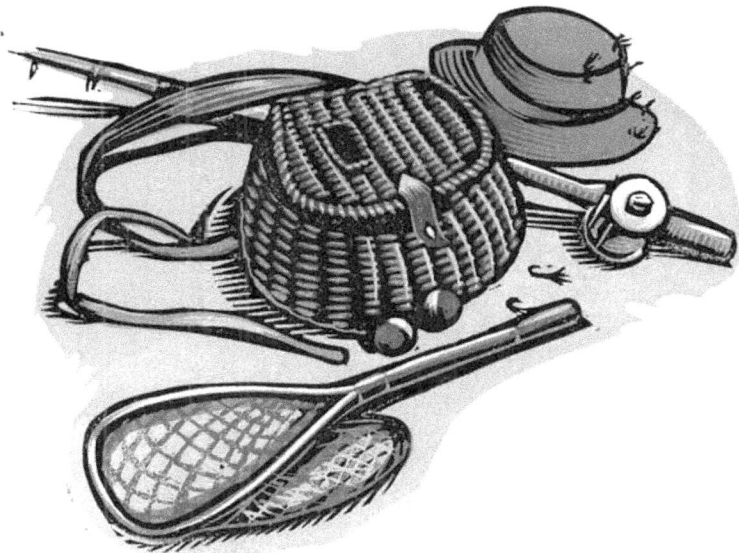

Rose, 75, felt depressed after she moved into an apartment. Not only had she given up her house to move to a small, dark apartment, but her health was getting worse. Her eyes were so bad, she couldn't read or sew. It seemed to her that her family harped nonstop about her drinking. Rose felt like telling them all to jump in a lake.

However, six months after her move, Rose found that her life had improved considerably. The eye specialist said her vision would probably not deteriorate further. She'd met her neighbors in the apartment building, so she didn't feel as dependent on her family for social outings. She started thinking about her health and the amount of alcohol that she'd been drinking. Maybe she should cut back. Six months later, she talked to her family doctor.

ॐ

Assessment

Screening instruments and measures of dependency or problem use may not be appropriate for older adults, because older adults may have problems with substance use at a much lower level of use than other age groups.

Usually, the assessment process is best done over a series of visits. Asking about substance use, particularly alcohol use, may seem intrusive and may be better left until you have developed a relationship with the older client and an appropriate opportunity presents itself rather than during a single structured interview. The older adult may not want to, or be able to, complete structured tests or forms.

The initial focus should always be on the person's immediate concern(s). These concerns need to be addressed as part of engaging the client in a process of change and developing a trusting relationship.

The type of information required will also differ from what is required from younger clients. Your work with older adults will have a greater focus on daily living and physical and social activities (see Table 3, Asking Older Adults about Substance Use).

TABLE 3: Asking Older Adults about Substance Use

Areas to include	Questions to ask
Sensory function	How well does the client see or hear (e.g., read labels on medication containers, books, newspapers)? Has the sense of taste been lost?
Mobility	Can the client move inside and outside, walk without aids, bathe and dress independently, shop for himself or herself?
Living environment and lifestyle	Is the client happy in his or her living situation? Have there been housing problems because of substance use? Can the client maintain his or her living environment? Does the environment have fire hazards or sanitation problems? Is it close enough to stores, buses, etc.? Does the client go out? How often does he or she see other people?

Losses	Has the client lost family, friends, a treasured pet, physical health (e.g., hearing, sight), a job or a home?
Diet	What are the client's eating habits (i.e., does he or she eat alone)? Does the client have a good appetite/enjoy food? How is food prepared and stored?
Mental condition	Is the client experiencing confusion, memory problems or psychiatric problems?
Physical health	Ask about sleeping patterns, weight change, disabilities and illnesses, medical supervision, dizziness, vision, hearing, foot care, digestion/elimination and dental problems.
Social support	Is there contact with family and friends? How much contact i there with other people? Does the client have close support versus simply acquaintances?
Literacy and speech	Does the client know how to read and write?
Alcohol and other drug use	How often and how much does he or she drink? Has the pattern of drinking changed (e.g., increased, decreased, periods of abstinence)? Has drinking affected other areas of life? What medications (prescription and non-prescription) are being used? How often, for how long, and why?

Source: Baron and Carver (1997).

Stages of Change Model

It is difficult to think about giving up things — whether the choice is giving up a home to move into an apartment or giving up something you enjoy because physical limitations make it too difficult. A period of mourning over loss is natural. When an older adult suffers a series of losses, it can be difficult to look positively on the world or to respond when people suggest more change, even if it is recognized that change may be in the person's best interests.

People of all ages need time, the right set of circumstances, and the right level of support if they are to make changes. The stereotype is that older adults are "set in their ways" or unable to change. A truer picture is that older adults, like people of all ages, are fully capable of change. But, like people of all ages, they must be at a stage where they are ready and feel able to start on a different course.

Regardless of age, each person is unique. Each person has a different learning style. Each has different ways of coping with problems. Each responds to treatment in different ways.

The stages of change model (Prochaska et al., 1994) is useful in thinking about how and why people change. The model helps you to recognize a client's attitude toward change and to decide the best strategy and tools to help the client at that stage. It is easier to stay positive and hopeful with clients if you understand that, even when people appear "stuck" or "in denial," their attitudes may be shifting even if their behavior has not yet changed. What sometimes seems like a sudden decision is often the result of a very long series of small decisions and a lot of thought about problems.

If, as a counsellor, you recognize that change can happen in slow steps, you are likely to be more comfortable offering a flexible, non-confrontational approach.

Although the examples given below in each stage refer to alcohol, the stages of change model is applicable to any life area in which the person is contemplating change. Also, people move back and forth between the stages and may be in different stages for different life areas.

STAGES OF CHANGE
Adapted from Addiction Research Foundation (1996).

Stage 1 — Precontemplation
"I don't want to change and I don't need to change."

Client Characteristics
- is not considering change: *"I drink. I like drinking."*
- does not recognize a need for change: *"I'm not addicted. I can quit anytime."*
- may be surprised by concern of family members or friends: *"I don't understand why you think I have a problem. It's their problem."*
- may not want to look at his or her substance use
- may participate in a limited manner or withdraw from counselling.

Counsellor Response
- establish rapport
- show respect and interest in what the client has to say
- give objective feedback
- set the stage by working on things that the client is interested in changing
- talk about how the client's substance use can have both positive and negative effects
- give the client some choices
- without being threatening, take appropriate opportunities to make the connection between alcohol and/or medication use and problems.

NOTE: If the client has said that his or her family and friends seem to think that there is a problem, this may allow you the opportunity to ask the following questions:
"Why do you think they are concerned?" or
"How do you know they are concerned?"
Look at the cause for concern as a forum to move the client to the contemplation stage.

Stage 2 — Contemplation
"I'd like to change. Maybe I will one day."

Client Characteristics
- is considering change, but is not ready to commit to change and may not believe that change is possible: *"I've thought about drinking less, but I enjoy it too much." "I'm too old to change. What good would it do?"*

- recognizes some of the negative effects of alcohol and medication use, but also feels substances play a positive role
- feels quitting would be too stressful right now.

Counsellor Response
- assist the client in moving beyond feelings of uncertainty
- help the client understand his or her mixed feelings about substance use
- explore positive and negative aspects of substance use in the client's life
- help the client recognize how substance use may not fit with her or his values, beliefs and image (e.g., *"I'm a good grandmother and I want to see my grandchildren often. Visits to my grandchildren are often cancelled because of my drinking."*)
- work with the client to show that change is possible.

NOTE: As a counsellor, you need to recognize that alcohol will have some positive effects for clients. For many clients, alcohol plays a role in coping with life's situations. It may be useful to discuss the issue of instant gratification versus delayed consequences with these clients.

Stage 3 — Preparation
"I want to change, but I haven't decided how to go about it."

Client Characteristics
- is getting ready to change
- feels more confident about the ability to change

- shifts focus from problems of the past and onto the future: *"If I stop drinking, I'll have more time to do other things that I really enjoy."*
- is searching for appropriate ways to turn wishes into actions
- talks to family and friends about the desired change and may ask for support
- may have already made some small changes.

Counsellor Response
- continue the process of working with the client to look at life and substance use in new ways
- encourage the client to focus on positive aspects of change and recognize fears about change
- help the client develop strategies to make changes
- provide concrete information about treatment choices and resources.

Stage 4 — Action
"I'm changing my behavior and replacing it with activities that are better for me."

Client Characteristics
- starts to change: *"I've cut down on the number of drinks I have each day."*
- expresses some urgency in wanting to begin the change process and see results right away: *"I need to get into a treatment program right now."*
- is changing his or her usual pattern of behavior
- is replacing substance use with healthier alternatives
- experiences an increase in self-esteem.

Counsellor Response

- support the client in coming to this point
- encourage the client's desire to change
- help the client develop confidence
- assist the client in accepting responsibility for making changes
- help the client understand his or her strengths and weaknesses to set realistic goals
- explore coping strategies
- help the client decide what healthy alternatives to pursue.

Stage 5 — Maintenance

"I'm keeping up my changed behavior and lifestyle."

Client Characteristics

- reinforces the change: *"I try to stay away from places where I used to drink."*
- integrates new skills and behaviors, including:
  - relating to others
  - learning how to ask for support
  - making decisions
  - exploring new ways of learning
  - finding alternative coping techniques: *"I had a long walk to help me relax."*

Counsellor Response

- help the client appreciate the benefits of change
- help the client develop a balanced lifestyle
- help the client explore alternatives, options and goals (e.g., volunteer work, hobbies)

- help the client identify potential relapse situations and plan coping strategies
- identify and reinforce positive changes in the client's behavior (e.g., ongoing support and or/individual or group counselling)
- help the client continue to build a new lifestyle
- refer the client to a self-help group
- explore coping strategies
- help the client decide what healthy alternatives to pursue.

Stage 6 — Termination
"I've changed for good!"

Client Characteristics
- has a more positive attitude and self-image
- is never tempted to resume substance use regardless of the situation or emotions that may have triggered use in the past: *"I no longer feel any desire to drink."*
- feels confident about coping with situations
- has an overall healthier lifestyle.

Counsellor Response
- congratulate the client on the good work in changing substance use
- help the client identify and avoid high-risk situations.

Relapse

Relapse is a return to problematic levels of substance use after a period of abstinence or reduced use. A relapse may be a brief episode (often called a lapse) or a more prolonged episode of substance use. Relapse may occur at any point in the recovery process.

If the client experiences a relapse, respond with empathy and help him or her cope with feelings of guilt by focusing on strengths, past achievements and things that give the client pleasure. If a person feels ashamed about relapsing, he or she is more likely to go back to the precontemplation phase. The client should be reminded that he or she has acquired new knowledge.

Help the client to view a relapse as an opportunity for further learning rather than as a failure. Work with the client to identify what triggered the relapse and what strategies can be useful to avoid one in the future. Assess the client's current needs. Dwelling on failure is counterproductive. Change happens when people feel strong enough to try again.

You can help clients take a proactive approach to relapse by helping to identify high-risk situations. People are most likely to relapse while experiencing one of the following situations (Annis, 1982):
• unpleasant emotions
• physical discomfort
• pleasant emotions
• testing personal control
• urges/cravings

• conflict with others
• social pressure
• pleasant times with others.

Ask which of these situations presents the greatest risk for the client? What situation is coming up next week that presents a high risk? What strategies help the client avoid substance use? What pleasant things can he or she do this week?

Section 5

How to Help

Pete, 77, decided to take his counsellor's advice. That Saturday, he went for a walk in the park. Then, he walked a little further and bought a newspaper. When his son, Jeff, stopped by that evening, Jeff noticed that his father talked about sports rather than his usual complaining about his aches and pains. Pete also seemed to have cut back on drinking. For the first time in a long time, Jeff saw a glimmer of his old father. It had been years since they'd seen a game together. On impulse, he suggested that he stay longer and that they watch the hockey game together. Pete was taken aback. Usually, Jeff couldn't get away fast enough.

Small changes can lead to bigger changes. This section describes how you can help bring about those changes. The approach described is holistic and client-centred, and it does not require the person to acknowledge a substance use problem in order to receive help.

In order to help a person with an alcohol or medication problem, it is useful to understand two terms that are common in the addictions field: denial and enabling.

Understanding Denial

"Denial" refers to people's tendency to minimize or deny the amount and/or effect of alcohol or medication in their lives. It is sometimes viewed as a barrier in the treatment of alcohol and medication problems.

Denial is a common mechanism that people use when faced with a situation that they feel they cannot change or that seems overwhelming. People often develop ways (such as anger and isolation) to avoid change and deal with the demands from others to change. For someone whose lifestyle has involved the use of alcohol and/or medication over many years, it is frightening to think of change. Underlying most denial is the belief that life without alcohol or medication would be either worse or impossible.

Although some addictions counsellors still feel that a client's denial of his or her substance use problems should be confronted head-on — such counsellors believe that's the only way that the client will recognize the life-threatening nature of the problem and take steps to change — this approach is not recommended.

Confrontation can become a barrier to change. If a person feels incapable of changing a situation or cannot see the value in change, confrontation may just lead to further denial. If we demand that clients "admit" to a problem before exploring possible solutions, then they may never see that a solution is possible. The best strategy in the face of denial may be to find ways to build the clients' self-confidence and success in achieving other changes leading to improved health. Within the context of making these changes, you may use appropriate opportunities to talk about how you see substance use affecting their health and lifestyle (e.g., how the problems they are experiencing may be related to the use of substances).

Just as older clients may experience denial, family members or even professionals may fail to recognize or deny substance use. Their denial may be related to the following situations:

- symptoms may be perceived as related to aging
- substance use may be perceived as "one of the few pleasures" in the older adult's life
- it may be considered "too late" for the older adult to benefit from change
- the person does not feel comfortable with a confrontational approach, but does not know any other way to deal with a substance use problem
- finding a tactful way to address substance use issues can be difficult, particularly for adult children who may not be used to talking to their parents about their behavior.

In some situations, people will feel relieved when the link is made between symptoms and the use of alcohol and/or medication. One day, the client or family may recognize that part of the symptoms that they associated with aging were, in fact, related to the use of medication or alcohol. With this recognition may come the awareness that change in behavior may result in a healthier, more satisfying life.

Enabling

"Enabling" commonly refers to activities or behaviors that "allow" a person to continue to use substances in a harmful manner. People close to the person with the problem are often the "enablers." The terms enabling and enabler have often been used to blame people. However, it is more useful to think of enabling as the desire to help a person without realizing that, by doing so, the person with the problem does not have to experience the consequences of substance use.

Common examples of enabling include covering up for a person and pretending that he or she is sick, when, in fact, the person is drinking; continuing to provide the person with alcohol; attributing forgetfulness to an age-related memory problem when it is due to an alcohol-related blackout.

If you have the opportunity to work with close friends or family members who have been enabling a client, try to help them realize that it is usually in the client's best interest to experience the consequences of his or her substance use.

Individual Counselling and Support

At any stage in life, taking care of oneself has much to do with self-image, self-esteem and hopefulness about life. Individual counselling can be an opportunity to focus on the client in a positive way and to build a relationship. This section includes a number of comments by clients themselves about their experiences in counselling, taken from an evaluation of the LESA program (West & Graham, 1997).

"If I ever had any trouble, I'd trust my counsellor to help me out."

"Visiting with the counsellor makes me feel good."

"We often sit around and talk about writing and one thing or another. We don't deal with drinking all the time. We talk about all kinds of things."

— LESA participants

Individual counselling should take place in a location most convenient for the client. Initially, at least, counselling for older adults is often provided in their own homes. This may address barriers created by mobility problems and/or a client's reluctance to seek treatment. The home can also provide clues that may not be apparent in an office setting, such as how chaotic the client's life might be or the stress in family relationships. Finally, an at-home visit gives the client a chance to be a host and have a sense of control over the relationship, something that may have been long missing from the person's life.

Individual counselling should proceed at the client's pace and issues should be dealt with as the client wishes. The counsellor's role is to work with the client to identify health issues, solve problems, support, encourage and provide resources to help the client make changes to improve his or her life.

When an older adult with whom you have contact appears to have social or health problems related to alcohol or psychoactive medication use, there are many ways for you to help that person. Through counselling and support visits, you strive to build the client's trust and confidence.

BUILD TRUST AND CONFIDENCE: THE THERAPEUTIC RELATIONSHIP

Your work begins by developing a therapeutic relationship with the older adult. The therapeutic relationship has two goals: first, for the client to develop trust and confidence in your ability to help him or her; and second, for you to get to know the person well enough to determine whether and how you can best work with him or her.

It is important to understand the client's situation:
• from his or her perspective
• from your own professional observations
• from information obtained from staff of other agencies
  or family members (with the client's written consent).

Listening and observing are essential to any activity that you do with the client. The focus must be on the client's needs and interests. In addition to learning the facts of the person's life, it is important to learn the client's feelings about, and the level of importance attached to, those facts.

As you develop a therapeutic relationship, it can take some time before the older adult is ready to consider making any changes. Helping with immediate problems of most concern to the client is often a starting point to building trust and confidence in you as someone who cares and can help. For example, a client may need help with a sick pet or minor household repairs, or just a chance to have a cup of tea and a talk. Offering practical help allows you further opportunity to get to know the person, his or her strengths and methods of coping with stress.

One way to think of the therapeutic relationship is in terms of a partnership. You wish to offer your professional skills, knowledge and support to the client to help that person make changes that will improve his or her health. You work together to identify and achieve changes in lifestyle and attitudes that will address alcohol and medication problems and improve the client's overall health.

As the therapeutic relationship develops, you may be concerned that the client is becoming overly dependent on you, particularly if he or she has little contact or support from family or friends. This can be alleviated by continually reinforcing the client's success in making changes. In addition, anticipate and try to prepare for potential setbacks or relapses so the client can become confident about his or her ability to make changes when you are not there to provide support.

The client also needs to know what to expect from you in this relationship. You must be honest about ways in which you are able to help as well as those in which you are not. For example, you could try the following statements:

"I am only able to meet with you twice a month. If something urgent comes up between visits, please call me."

"I am not trained to do family counselling, so I would like to suggest the names of some family counsellors who might help you with your relationship with your husband."

"I won't be able to stay and visit with you if you have been drinking before our scheduled visit. But I will always reschedule. I value our visits."

A good therapeutic relationship is essential to the success of counselling. Your responsibility in this relationship is to offer your knowledge, skills, time and support to assist the client in changing attitudes, environmental situations and behaviors that will lead to better overall health.

IDENTIFY REASONS FOR CHANGE

This work needs to be done in partnership with the client. Active listening is one of the major skills used in helping the client to reflect on his or her life and identify areas where change might bring more comfort or meaning. Observing the client's interests, strengths and circumstances and reflecting your observations back to the client helps identify areas where healthy changes in lifestyle or attitude might be attempted.

BUILD CONFIDENCE IN THE ABILITY TO CHANGE

Both you and the client may feel overwhelmed when faced with multiple problems in the client's life. Where do you begin? Consider some of the following steps:

• Review the stages of change model described in the previous section. It will help you understand the client's perspective on his or her problem and ways that you might intervene.

• Help the client choose areas for change that have a realistic chance of success.

• Encourage the client to break the change process into small steps. A client who wants to become less isolated might try going to the mall and having a cup of coffee as a first step to leaving his or her apartment. When the client feels comfortable doing that, he or she might then consider another activity more directly involved with people. A client who wants to increase his or her energy might consider a walk around the block or a small change in diet as first steps.

Evaluate why intentions to change behavior worked or didn't work. Help the client recognize and enjoy feelings of success. Help review why things didn't work out and identify alternative steps for achieving change.

SOLVE PROBLEMS, OFFER SUPPORT AND IDENTIFY RESOURCES

Much of the activity of the individual counsellor revolves around helping to solve problems, offering support, identifying and assisting the client to access resources. Following are a few activities you may use to help older adults:

• Work on solvable problems:

  • **Health, mobility issues:** How can you help the client to achieve health objectives? What community resources do you know about that could support the client? What special transportation resources, such as volunteer drivers, exist?

  • **Literacy:** Does the client need help with basic literacy skills? Arrange links to literacy programs designed for older adults in the community.

  • **Isolation, loneliness:** Help the client access family or community resources. Again, know what is available in the community and help remove barriers to accessing resources. Advocate for the client when needed. Accompany the client the first time he or she attends new activities as a way to offer support. Is there a friendly visitor organization?

- **Feelings of worthlessness or a lack of purpose:** What kinds of activities does the client consider worthwhile? What activities or interests did the client enjoy in the past? Explore his or her dreams. Is there something he or she always wanted to do but couldn't?

- **Grief, depression:** Has the client been medically assessed for clinical depression? Does the client have someone to talk with about how he or she feels? What groups exist to help with specific issues? Assess your own understanding of grief and depression. Listen and acknowledge the client's feelings.

- **Spirituality:** How comfortable is the person with himself or herself? Is he or she having difficulty coming to terms with getting older — with death?

- **Conflicts arising from past alcohol and/or medication use:** How can the person re-connect with family or friends? How can housing or financial difficulties be resolved?

• Offer encouragement and assistance to try a different approach when something doesn't work. Emphasize that if something hasn't worked this time, it may work next time and that alternatives can be tried. Change is about learning what works and what doesn't work.

• Recall past examples of change and use them to encourage the client and as a learning opportunity. Use comments such as the following:

*"When you stopped smoking after your surgery last year,
how did you do it?"*

*"You really seemed to enjoy that exercise class you went to
this winter at the community centre. Do you think they might
have summer activities you would enjoy?"*

• Identify resources to help the person change.

*"Do you think your son would be able to drive you to
visit your friend?"*

*"Did you know that there is a bus that takes seniors to
the grocery store?"*

• Find out what volunteer resources are available in the community and explore the client's comfort in using such services.

• Use methods such as role-playing to increase the likelihood
of success for the client who must talk to another person to get
something that he or she needs.

*"Let's walk through what might happen when you talk to
the doctor about your Valium... or to the housing people
about getting an apartment."*

WORK ON PROBLEMS WITH ALCOHOL AND/OR PSYCHOACTIVE MEDICATION

Reducing or eliminating alcohol or psychoactive medication
use can also be done in small steps. In your early contacts with
clients, some may be ready to talk about their substance use and

set achievable goals for reducing or eliminating use. However, for many people, it will take time to feel comfortable in acknowledging a problem related to substance use. In these situations, there are many ways to broach the subject of alcohol and/or medication use *in the context of an established therapeutic relationship.*

• Use opportunities to raise the issue of alcohol or psychoactive medication use in a non-threatening manner.

"Sometimes drinking makes people forget they did things. Perhaps you forgot that you arranged to see your friend because you were drinking when she called."

"Do you think your son doesn't want you to babysit the grandchildren because he is concerned you will be drinking when you are with them?"

"When I come to visit you and you are drinking, it is difficult to talk to you. Perhaps your daughter feels like that too."

"Sometimes the kind of medication you are using can make people feel dizzy. Perhaps that might be why you fell."

"It seems when I visit and you are drinking, you seem sad. Did you know that alcohol can make you feel depressed?"

"Your landlord said he may have to ask you to leave because the neighbors get upset when you are drinking. How can I help you to make sure that doesn't happen again?"

• When the client feels comfortable talking about alcohol or psychoactive medication use, help him or her assess the amount being used, when substances are used, and the positive and negative effects of substance use. Ask questions such as the following:

"How does drinking help you feel better?"

"How are you feeling or what is happening before you have a drink?"

"Under what circumstances do you take your medication?"

"What is happening on the days that you drink less?"

• Encourage clients to use a monitoring log to record alcohol or psychoactive medication use (see Appendix B). Monitoring consumption helps clients to identify how much and in what situations they drink or take psychoactive medication. This information can then be used to help them identify strategies to deal with high-risk situations for substance use.

• Some clients may not be willing to consider abstinence initially, even though this would seem a desirable goal. However, they may be willing to try to reduce their use and see this as a more achievable goal. They should be encouraged and supported in their efforts to do this. Any reduction in the amount consumed per drinking episode, or any reduction in the days per week when drinking occurs, is a step toward helping the client build confidence and gain control over that aspect of his or her life. If clients are successful in reducing their substance use, this may improve their health as well as reinforce success. However, if they find it too difficult to maintain reduced levels of use, they may be willing to try to eliminate substance use altogether.

• If the client is attempting to totally withdraw from alcohol or psychoactive medication, it is important to remember the need for specialized help (e.g., a physician to work with the client on a regimen to taper medication use, or a detoxification centre to observe and support the client while withdrawing from high levels of alcohol use).

CLOSURE

Because of the multiplicity of problems experienced by the older client, it may be difficult for you to determine the best time to stop seeing that person. The following factors may be considered:

• The client's needs and desires:

 • The client is satisfied with improved health and does not wish further involvement.

 • The client still has identified needs but does not want further involvement.

In the following situations, you might decide to refer the client to another counsellor or specialized service:

 • The client still has identified needs or wants further support but shows no sign of making any changes. Have you tried other approaches? Would the client respond to a different counsellor?

- The client isn't involved with any other services, and you have serious concerns about his or her ability to cope (e.g., the client may become suicidal). Could a psychiatric referral or other supports help the client and allow you to continue your work with him or her? Should your work be postponed until the client is more stable?

• The counsellor's abilities or limits in helping the client:

  - The client has needs outside the area of expertise of the counsellor and requires a referral to another service.

  - The counsellor is limited by the mandate of his or her agency or program.

  - There is not a "good fit" between the counsellor and the client. It is important to recognize that the development of a therapeutic relationship or partnership is essential in helping the client. The client must feel that the counsellor is working for his or her best interests. Equally, the counsellor must feel that he or she can help the client. Particularly when dealing with substance use problems, it is important that counsellors themselves not have any unresolved issues around substance use. This might include the counsellor's own previous history of problem substance use or that of a family member. Either could interfere with the ability to provide professional help and support to the client. If these elements are interfering with a therapeutic relationship, the client should have the opportunity to see another counsellor.

Group Support

At programs such as LESA and COPA, support groups have always been an integral part of the program. Group meetings evoke feelings of acceptance and belonging. Feeling comfortable in a group setting and social networking can rekindle feelings of self-worth. Groups provide a place to be inspired by and learn from others who have been successful in making changes, as well as a place to work out one's own problems with the help of peers. Joining others in group discussions and/or group activities can be important in reinforcing lifestyle change.

• Group experiences increase feelings of comfort with others in a group or social setting.

"There's no pressure at all... nobody says that you can't do this or you can't do that or anything else. Actually, if you still want to drink, you're going to have a drink. There's nobody going to hit you on the head."

– LESA participant

Feeling comfortable and accepted is important at any age. Some people are natural joiners and like being part of a group. Others are more hesitant joiners. For most older adults, being with people in the same age group adds to the feeling of comfort in group meetings. Most prefer to be with others who share similar histories and exposure to world events. Younger people are seen to have different problems because they are at a different stage in their lives. Older clients often feel that they do not share in young people's problems, particularly illegal drug use.

LESA and COPA staff have found that men and women often prefer separate meetings because they have separate and distinct needs and issues. In addition, women are sometimes inhibited from speaking in mixed groups.

• Group experiences encourage a sharing of experiences.

"I felt like I was the only one in this position, and knowing that there were others out there and other people — decent people, loving, kind, ordinary people like me, you know — having the same problem, that really made me feel a lot better about everything."

— LESA participant

Hearing what other people have to say about their problems can be helpful. People can learn from other group members how to develop strategies to avoid alcohol at events such as weddings. At the same time, not discussing alcohol can be important. A counsellor's willingness to have group discussions on issues other than alcohol and medication use is a way to acknowledge the many aspects of people's lives and not just focus on problems.

• Group experiences develop a social network.

"If it was all very, very serious stuff, probably it wouldn't be as attractive to me. We always manage to have a laugh."

— LESA participant

Just as individual counselling evokes positive emotions, having
fun within a group is an incentive to keep coming and to stop
thinking about problems. Groups are an opportunity to socialize
in a relaxed setting and practise social skills. Having something
to look forward to — somewhere to go and have fun — is important for people at any age. Group meetings, facilitated by one
or two counsellors, provide the opportunity for clients to share
concerns and support one another. Discussions can cover a range
of issues from medication and health issues to housing and
finances. As well, miscellaneous topics allow clients to focus
on a world beyond their problems — from literacy and transportation to schools and volunteer work.

If specialized programs for older adults are not available in your
community, there are several options for facilitating group support
for the client. Can you or someone else from your agency partner
with a local addiction treatment agency to offer a group for older
adults? Are there other groups in the community offered by
specific services that might be suitable for the client? Would the
client be comfortable attending a regular outpatient addiction
treatment program?

NOTE: For further information about facilitating support groups
for older clients, see Bergin and Baron (1992).

Recreational Support

Recreational outings allow clients to have fun with others. This
is particularly important for clients who are socially isolated or
whose social life has been associated with drinking. Having fun,

experiencing pleasure and socializing with the opposite sex can be strong motivators to making changes in one's life so that the pleasant experiences can be repeated.

Again, are there resources within your own agency, or in partnership with an addiction treatment agency, that could offer occasional recreational outings for older clients with substance use problems? If not, what are the options available in the community and how can they be matched with the client's needs and interests?

Suggestions for a Healthier Lifestyle

Common sense ideas might help a client to develop a healthier lifestyle. Most suggestions are simple and straightforward enough. They have to do with focusing on the things a person can do to take control of his or her own health and to better enjoy life.

PSYCHOSOCIAL

Supportive social relationships and social networks are factors in helping people cope with stress, feelings of isolation or boredom, especially the boredom faced by some older adults after retirement. Older adults could benefit from any of the following:
• becoming a volunteer
• pursuing a hobby or taking a class
• going where there are people
• restarting a hobby that got put aside when they were too busy
• reconnecting with old friends
• getting out every day
• trying moderate exercise

- talking with a friend
- doing relaxation exercises
- playing favorite music
- adopting a pet
- keeping house plants
- understanding that symptoms of depression and anxiety can be treated.

SPIRITUAL

For some people, age can bring many losses. You can encourage clients to address these issues in their own ways. You could suggest that they try the following:

- talking with a friend
- talking with a religious leader or a counsellor
- reading books or listening to tapes
- joining a group that deals with life issues such as suicide or grief
- working for a worthwhile cause
- focusing on the good things in life.

PHYSICAL

Common sense health practices are important for older adults who may face physical limitations or health problems. The following suggestions could help address older clients' needs in three key areas: general health, pain management and sleep disturbances.

General Health

To enhance their overall health, older adults could try the following:

- joining an exercise class or "aquafit" class or mall-walking group

- spending a portion of the day outdoors
- eating regular well-balanced meals
- seeking help early; delays in diagnosing a problem can worsen the situation
- writing down their doctor's instructions to assure a proper health regimen
- writing down their own health plans for improving their health.

Pain Management

To cope with pain, older adults could try the following:
- taking an active role in understanding physical limitations and the ways to practise pain management
- gathering information or taking a course about specific health issues (e.g., arthritis)
- trying exercise, massage, or cold or hot compresses to reduce some types of pain
- asking their doctor about non-medication treatments.

Sleep Disturbances

Older adults who have trouble sleeping could try the following:
- making their bedroom more comfortable
- treating themselves to a warm bath
- drinking a glass of warm milk
- avoiding caffeine and other stimulants or spicy foods after 4 p.m.
- trying herbal teas
- avoiding alcohol in the evening
- avoiding worrying about their insomnia — and getting up and doing something until they are sleepy
- accepting that less sleep is needed as people age
- avoiding daytime napping

- listening to relaxing music
- establishing bedtime rituals and regular sleep habits
- counting sheep (it really works)!

Summary

It is important to recognize each client's readiness to change. Often, older adults have come into contact with many counsellors throughout their lives. Some counsellors may have been confrontational. Some may have given up. The first task is to understand clients' perspectives and use that as a stepping stone to help them improve their lives. The key is to look at alcohol and medication use primarily as a health issue. Build a relationship first, and then explore health issues. Be ready to make the connection between alcohol and/or medication use when the time is right.

Section 6

Common Questions

Common Questions

Q. How do I ask a client about drinking?

A. Questions that elicit a response tend to be those asked in a direct, non-judgmental way. As health professionals, counsellors are comfortable asking questions such as: *"Do you smoke?"* and *"How many cigarettes per day do you smoke?"* The same approach can be used with alcohol.

"In a regular week, how many days do you drink? On those days, how many drinks do you have?"

Of course, some people may not yet be willing to respond to these types of questions (e.g., *"I don't drink"* or *"That's none of your concern."*) .

How can you respond? As a counsellor, you can accept that the client may be in the precontemplative stage. Keep in mind that the goal is to form a therapeutic relationship with the client. You need to consider what is to be gained by asking these kinds of questions. You may be feeling "stuck" yourself, particularly if there is evidence that the client is drinking. Self-awareness is essential when you are with a client. However, experience has proven that accepting each client's particular stage helps to maintain the therapeutic relationship. Work on the problems identified by the client. There will be other opportunities to address the client's substance use.

The main goal at this stage is to assess the situation and develop a trusting relationship — it's crucial to engage the client.

Q. If the client does not want to talk about drinking or is in the precontemplation stage, how do you address substance use?

A. You can ask other questions:

"What stresses are you experiencing now?" This is a chance for the client to prioritize.

"How are you coping?" This is a chance to identify coping strategies.

"Are others concerned about your drinking? Why do you think that is?" This type of question elicits the client's perspective and provides a reasoning that is already accepted by the client.

"What are your concerns?" Housing? Health? Boredom? Despair? Depression? You are helping the client look at his or her quality of life. What can be done to address the client's needs? Is there an area where you, as the counsellor, can be involved? Who else may become involved?

Q. The client is visibly intoxicated when you arrive. What do you do?

A. Focus on the situation and address it: *"Since you have been drinking, this isn't going to be a useful visit for either of us. However, I will be back next week at this time. Here is the date and time on my business card."*

If the client has had a drink but is still communicating well, you may stay for a short time with the goal of identifying what led to the drinking — clients sometimes "fortify" themselves with alcohol to cope with a counsellor's visit.

If a client is consistently drinking before your visits, there are several approaches. *"I see you are always drinking when I come. What would be a better time of day for you?"* or *"I'm not comfortable being here. When you are drinking, we don't have a productive visit. May I come first thing in the morning, and then we can have coffee together?"*

Changing the time of day has two practical advantages:

1. You have some control and input by asking the client the reasons he or she has for starting the day drinking, and you can help the client develop strategies to delay that first drink. *"What do you think is a reasonable time of day to have a drink?"*

2. Drinking is clearly identified as problematic when it interferes with important events such as the counsellor's visits. This allows for negotiation as to acceptable behavior. Each situation will differ. Be creative and non-judgmental. Be kind, fair and firm.

Q. A client asks you to pour (or bring) a drink. What should you do?

A. This is a difficult situation, but a clear one. *"My reason for being here is to help you work through some recent problems. Since we only have this short time once a week, it's important to me that drinking is not happening while I'm here."*

Q. The client seems confused and may be drinking a little. He or she has been on Valium® for over 15 years and has poor short-term memory. How do I intervene?

A. Do you know the purpose of the Valium®? Is it even necessary? What could it be masking? Can the client live without it? What role does alcohol play? How often is the client drinking? How much is he or she drinking? What strengths can you identify?

By identifying all the psychosocial issues covered in assessment, you can evaluate the problem areas. With the client's permission, can you approach his or her physician to see if there's a link between the client's confusion and the use of Valium® and alcohol? Here is an area where you can enlist outside help. Addiction treatment centres may be able to provide the client's medical practitioner with guidelines.

Q. A client always tells me that he or she has an occasional glass of sherry when his or her son visits. I've noticed empty beer cases stacked in the hall, and the client says they were left by the son. Given the client's memory problems, I have no sense of the actual situation. What do I do?

A. Getting to the truth can sometimes be frustrating and time-consuming. Work with the area that you know and you agree on — the occasional sherry that the client acknowledges. Use this as a starting point for discussion with the client.

Q. A client asks, "How much do you drink?" How do I respond?

A. Since the relationship is built on honesty and trust, it is fine to be honest. Since the idea is to focus on the client's needs, a simple, honest answer and a return to focus on the client is appropriate. You could say: *"I believe in moderation. How about you?"*

Section 7

Client Profiles

Client Profiles

The following client profiles were developed in consultation with counsellors who work with older adults in client-centred environments. The profiles are based on real cases and the advice provided represents the views of the counsellor involved and a team of health care professionals. The profiles are meant only as a guide to how counsellors might approach similar situations.

Client Profile 1: Ann

I'm a pastor in a parish in a small town in northern Ontario. Ann, age 70, has been a parishioner in this parish all her life. I have known her since I came here seven years ago. I also knew her husband, George, who died two years ago. George was a heavy drinker. Ann's two adult children are also heavy drinkers. Ann had alcohol problems when she was in her 40s, but she managed to avoid severe problems by going back to work. She worked until she was 65.

On my occasional pastoral visits during the last two years, I have become aware that Ann is very lonely and does not have a lot of close friends in town. She describes how the drinking behavior of her husband and sons kept her from socializing with others. She is also concerned about the sexual orientation of both her sons, who live in the city, and she believes that possible sexual abuse by a male friend of the family might be a factor. She says that she can't hold her head up in town and she feels ashamed of her family, yet she loves them very much. She sometimes comments that she hasn't been a very good mother. She drank heavily when the children were young, and then she dealt with her problems by going to work and not being at home when the children might have needed her.

I have noticed during the past year that, when my visits are in the late afternoon, Ann has usually been drinking before my arrival. She offers me a beer. Even when I request tea, she continues to drink beer herself. Ann has missed coming to church two or three times over the past couple of months, which is unusual for her.

There is a grief group in our parish and I wish that I could get Ann to attend. She would soon find out that she is not alone in her problems. There is a lot of drinking in this town and the subject comes up quite frequently. However, Ann only responds that she couldn't join a group and that she would never want to talk to outsiders about her problems.

There are no formal treatment programs in this community. Ann says that she would never want people in town to think that she is an alcoholic. Besides, she says that she isn't really drinking that much yet.

I can continue to visit Ann occasionally, but I am concerned about her isolation and her apparent increase in alcohol use. She won't really talk to me much about the drinking. My concerns are based on my observations. What can I do? Where can I send her for help?

ASSESSMENT

Although a formal assessment was not done, the pastor has recognized Ann's strengths and difficulties. It sounds as though Ann trusts him, because she has told him a lot of personal things. In essence, the work of the assessment period — to identify

strengths and problems and to develop a trusting relationship —
has been done. One aspect that is unclear is the extent to which
Ann recognizes this work and the degree to which she is able
to, and wishes to, make some changes.

PROBLEMS

Ann has social, psychological and spiritual problems that are
affecting her quality of life. These problems involve many issues:
increased alcohol use, likely daily drinking; social isolation and
loneliness; and feelings of shame, guilt and remorse. She does
not feel close to her sons who are now living in the city and she
would like to see them more often. They do phone and visit occasionally. Ann apparently does not have strong ties with extended
family or friends who could support her. To date, Ann has not
seemed able to take any direct steps to change her situation.

STRENGTHS AND MOTIVATORS

Ann recognized an alcohol use problem in the past and was
successful in taking steps to remedy that problem. Ann has
successfully handled a job. She has insight into her feelings
(i.e., shame, guilt and remorse). She recognized that she has
difficulty dealing with her sons' sexual orientation. She has
maintained contact with both sons, as they have with her. She
has been able to form a relationship with her pastor and can
be open in expressing her situation.

DISCUSSION

Ann knows the havoc that alcohol can play. Dwelling on this will
only reinforce her negative feelings about herself. Instead, the
focus should be on the issues that are causing negative feelings
and using past successes to help her build strength to begin again.

As a counsellor, try asking questions such as the following:

"Was there a time that you drank less?"

"Do you think there was more stress in your life back then?"

"How does drinking help you now?"

"Are there any drawbacks to drinking that you can see?"

Such questions are meant to elicit the client's perspective and feelings about the issue.

"What stresses are you experiencing now?"

This question allows the client to prioritize.

"How are you coping?"

This is an invitation to identify coping strategies, which may include drinking. (The client may say: *"I am so worried that I can't sleep. My mind won't stop running. I know a couple of beers will help."*)

PATTERN OF SUBSTANCE USE

According to the part of Section 2 that covers life patterns of substance use, Ann has characteristics of both *intermittent* and *late onset* problems. Ann had alcohol problems in the past but was able to stop drinking and live, for an extended period, without the negative effects of alcohol. Later in life, several things happened that probably influenced her to start drinking heavily again, including the death of her husband, her concerns about her sons, her social isolation and loneliness.

STAGES OF CHANGE

Ann appears to be in the contemplation stage with regard to drinking and in the preparation stage with regard to other problems
(as shown by her willingness to talk about them). With regard to drinking, she says that she doesn't want to go to Alcoholics Anonymous (AA) and she isn't drinking too much "yet." Also, she knows that she doesn't want to talk to others about her problems. This allows some opening to further explore her drinking and seek other solutions more acceptable to Ann. She handled her drinking by going to work before; maybe other activities, such as volunteer work, could again offer her a solution.

ACTION PLAN

Ann's most pressing problem, from her point of view, seems to be her relationship with her sons. She would like to be closer to them. She also has feelings of guilt and remorse about her role as a mother. Yet, her sons are still in contact with her, so this seems a good place to start. If the pastor can visit her more frequently, he may be able to help her explore her feelings of guilt.

"You have mentioned that you were drinking rather heavily at one time in your life but that you were able to stop when you went back to work. Can you tell me a little more about that? How do you think this may have helped your sons? How did you cope under the circumstances?"

Concentrate on her strengths and the practical ways to get closer to her sons. Probably, it would be helpful for her to explore her own feelings about different sexual orientations.

"There's a lot of confusion about different sexual orientations today. We seem to be learning a lot about how people differ. Have you been able to sort out how you feel about different sexual orientations? I know that the church has been quite rigid in the past, but it is beginning to reflect on the issue also."

The pastor should ask himself if he is a suitable person to help Ann work through this issue. What are his own feelings and views on different sexual orientations? Since he is a trusted clergyman, the pastor would be in an excellent position to help Ann with her feelings of guilt and remorse. When Ann begins to feel better about herself, the pastor might be more successful in getting her involved in the grief support group or some other activity of her choosing.

Given that the relationship is friendly and trusting, the pastor should feel free to express his concern about what he sees as increased drinking without expectations of immediate change on Ann's part. The key is to work with her in areas of change that she sees as important, taking every opportunity to comment on her strengths as they are revealed. At the same time, it's important to continue to increase Ann's awareness about her alcohol use and how it might prevent her from achieving her goals.

OTHER RESOURCES AND ACTIVITIES
- Family physician, especially if there is a long-standing relationship
- Literature on spiritual topics, especially related to reducing guilt and remorse

- Physical exercise, walking or classes where she can work alone in a group but feel less threatened than she would in a discussion group.

Client Profile 2: Paul

As part of the home-care team, I was asked to visit with Paul, 63, whose living situation had deteriorated to the extent that the volunteers from Meals-on-Wheels (MOW) had serious concerns regarding his welfare. Paul had a long history of heavy drinking, both socially and at work. On several occasions, he had been jailed for impaired driving. He also reported a family history of alcoholism. In recent years, his drinking had become more solitary. He drank alone in his apartment, no longer worked and had no social contacts or satisfying leisure pursuits.

His poor health seemed to limit his activities. He apparently drank in response to his loneliness, depression and boredom. However, he had been abstinent for several periods in the past (for up to two years). When drinking, Paul typically reported consuming two to three drinks per day; but, based on his appearance, mood and visible empty bottles, it is likely that he was under-reporting his consumption.

While drinking, Paul was most inactive and he neglected self-care and the care of his apartment. In this case, the self-neglect was severe — rotting food, roaches, maggots and garbage brought complaints from his landlord. He neglected nutrition and would often leave meals from Meals-on-Wheels untouched. He had a number of physical health problems (hiatus hernia with esophageal strictures, seizure disorder, chest pains) and was reluctant to seek medical help (especially when drinking). He did not take his medications — other than analgesics, which the worker thought he might be abusing.

∂

ASSESSMENT

As Paul had not requested a home-care assessment or assistance from a health care professional, there was an immediate problem. As the identifying agency was Meals-on-Wheels, it was proposed that MOW staff simply ask Paul: *"May the home-care worker come to check your nutritional needs next week?"* Paul agreed. His response was that the agency was interfering, but he didn't care. The first hurdle had been crossed.

The initial visit lasted about 45 minutes. Paul was a reluctant participant. He clearly stated that he had no need for help and that the visit was a waste of taxpayers' money. Following the agenda of the referring agency, MOW, a discussion of Paul's diet, appetite and tolerance of food seemed neutral ground. This led to a discussion about general health (usually a rewarding topic for both parties) and a direct opportunity for education on nutrition and the use of medication — incidentally leading to a discussion about alcohol use.

Paul was also angry with his landlord — a problem with possibilities for discussion. How important was it to Paul to maintain his independence? What steps could he take to ensure his independence? How had he managed in the past? Could Paul and his home-care worker work through the pros and cons? *"Wow, Paul,*

we've covered a lot of ground — may I come back next week?
I'd like to help you develop some of these areas."

PROBLEMS

Paul has acknowledged health problems but shows a marked reluctance to work on them. His attitude is: *"An old dog can't learn new tricks." "What difference will it make?" "I've managed so far."*

STRENGTHS AND MOTIVATORS

Paul is willing to communicate freely about a range of issues. This is important when the counsellor and client are looking at making changes. Let's look at Paul's drinking. Paul has had periods of abstinence. He can be asked: *"How did you do that?"* If you can help Paul recognize his successes and identify in detail how he achieved those successes, you can ask him to use the same strategies again. There are no new concepts or skills to be learned! The scenario could look like this:

Counsellor: *"So, Paul, you succeeded in not drinking for a huge block of time in 1978. That's quite an achievement. It would be helpful for me to know how you did that. How did you go from day to day without drinking?"*

Paul: *"I don't know. I just did."*

Counsellor: *"Do you remember what was happening in your life that led to your decision to stop drinking?"*

Paul: *"Well, I was ill for a while."*

NOTE: Paul could identify any issue: eviction, when his spouse left, his legal issues, or when his family refused to speak to him. Regardless of the issue, Paul took action — he stopped drinking. As a counsellor, you can use this information as a starting point. Try to determine what motivated Paul to stop drinking, and work from there.

Counsellor: *"I hear that you coped extremely well with that stress. Now, you have different concerns in your life. What would you see as a benefit now if you cut back on your drinking for a while?"*

Paul: *"Maybe the landlord would leave me alone (or my stomach pains would go away)."*

Counsellor: *"Yes, that's possible. What are the things that make it difficult for you to stop drinking?"*

Paul: *"I like drinking. I don't want to go through withdrawal. I have nothing better to do. I just sit here all day. I can even get beer delivered. How many more reasons do you need?"*

Counsellor (with humor): *"Well, Paul, this is going to be a tough haul for you to drink less. Can we work on it together?"*

DISCUSSION

Clearly, Paul is not ready to make major lifestyle changes. However, he may be able to respond to some gentle questioning, which could plant a seed for the future.

"Was there any time that you have not been drinking?
How was that different for you?"

PATTERN OF SUBSTANCE USE

According to the part of Section 2 that covers life patterns of substance use, Paul has the characteristics of *early onset* problems. This has major implications on how a treatment plan can be developed. What differentiates the client with early onset problems from other clients are the following points: 1) the client's health has been noticeably changed due to drinking; and 2) the client may be more willing to discuss change, but his or her experience of withdrawal and possible failure at treatment can make the client resistant to try again. Paul also shows signs of misuse of medication.

STAGES OF CHANGE

Paul might be considered in the precontemplation stage. Although he has talked about his drinking, he has not indicated changing. Others can see the problem, but he can't.

ACTION PLAN

Based on knowledge of Paul's situation, a plan of action can be developed. The counsellor will act in the capacity of motivator, resource provider and advocate. Generally, these are areas within the mandate and philosophy of agencies that provide health care. Thus, they become part of the treatment plan.

With Paul's consent, advocacy might include discussions with Meals-on-Wheels and his landlord to let them know that he is working on change. In approaching the landlord, the counsellor hopes to obtain a little space and time.

"I recognize your dilemma. You have other tenants to consider. Can you allow me some time? Then, either the situation will improve or alternative accommodation will be found."

OTHER RESOURCES AND ACTIVITIES

- Physician (most of Paul's physical health problems are treatable or can be eased)
- Seniors' clubs, volunteering, hobbies, walking, riding the local bus, libraries
- Family and friends
- The client has personal strengths that have not yet been investigated.

Appendix
A

Additional Information

Additional Information

Addiction Clinical Consultation Service (ACCS)
This service provides information for Ontario health and social
services professionals and expert advice on issues such as medical
complications of drug and alcohol use, drug interactions, management of clients with addiction problems, counselling for individuals, couples and families.
Phone: 1-888-720-ACCS

Addiction Research Foundation (ARF), a Division of the Centre
for Addiction and Mental Health Toll-free confidential information about alcohol and other drugs is available from ARF's
Information Centre. The ARF Web site has a comprehensive list
of sources for material on issues related to addiction.
Phone: 1-800-INFO-ARF
http://www.arf.org

Canadian Centre on Substance Abuse (CCSA)
The Canadian Centre on Substance Abuse provides information
on the nature, extent and consequences of substance use and
supports and assists organizations involved in treatment, prevention and educational programming.
Phone: 613-235-4048   Fax: 613-235-8101
http://www.ccsa.ca

Community Older Persons Alcohol (COPA) Program
The program provides an outreach service to older adults with alco-
hol- and other drug-related problems. It is designed to help individuals identify lifestyle problems, reduce or eliminate substance use, and
develop healthy alternatives. It serves the West Toronto area. COPA
provides telephone consultation and home detoxification services.
Phone: 416-516-2982   Fax: 416-516-2984

Drug and Alcohol Registry of Treatment (DART)
DART provides information for professionals and the public about treatment options and availability in Ontario.
Phone: 1-800-565-8603

Health Canada
The Health Canada Web site has current information on research initiatives, community projects and innovative programming from all levels of government, non-governmental organizations and the private sector.
http://www.hwc.ca

Lifestyle Enrichment for Senior Adults (LESA)
The program offers in-home counselling and group support for senior adults experiencing problems related to the use of alcohol and other psychoactive drugs, and to aging. The focus is on lifestyle change and overall improvement in health. LESA provides services in English and French in the Ottawa-Carleton area.
Phone: 613-563-4799   Fax: 613-563-0163

Local Addiction Services
Check local listings in your telephone book or phone the Drug and Alcohol Registry of Treatment's (DART's) toll-free number, listed above, for information.

Substance Abuse Network of Ontario (SANO)
This interactive computer network features addiction-related information, including news and events, jobs, and programs and partnerships.
http://sano.arf.org

Appendix B

Monitoring Form

Monitoring Form

WEEKLY DRINKING GOAL   <u>15 drinks</u>   **(maximum amount)**

Drinking Goal for the Week: 15 drinks

Day	Drink/Amount	Where/Situation	Medications/ Amount
Mon.	2 bottles of beer	at home/playing cards with friends	Tylenol®
Tues.	2 bottles of beer	alone at home	Tylenol®
Wed.	4 bottles of beer/ glass of wine	out with friends	Nerve pill at bedtime
Thurs.	didn't drink		Nerve pill at bedtime
Fri.	2 bottles of beer	alone at home	
Sat.	3 bottles of beer	while watching TV	
Sun.	3 bottles of beer	while watching TV	Tylenol®

TOTAL   16 beers, 1 glass of wine

Medications currently being used:

Rivotril® for sleep problems

Tylenol #1® for occasional headaches

Coumadin® for stroke some years ago

References

Monitoring Form

WEEKLY DRINKING GOAL _____ (maximum amount)

Day	Drink/Amount	Where/Situation	Medications/ Amount
Mon.			
Tues.			
Wed.			
Thurs.			
Fri.			
Sat.			
Sun.			

TOTAL

Medications currently being used:

_____

_____

_____

References

Addiction Research Foundation. (1995). *Promoting Choice: A Community Action Guide for the Safe Use of Alcohol and Medications by Older Adults*. Toronto: Addiction Research Foundation.

Addiction Research Foundation. (1996). *The Hidden Majority: A Guidebook on Alcohol and Other Drug Issues for Counsellors Who Work with Women*. Toronto: Addiction Research Foundation.

Addiction Research Foundation. (1997). *Alcohol and Your Health, It's a Question of Balance, Low-Risk Drinking Guidelines*. Toronto: Addiction Research Foundation.

Addiction Research Foundation, Lifestyle Enrichment for Senior Adults & Community Older Persons Alcohol Program. (1993). *Alternatives: Prevention and Intervention for Alcohol and Drug Problems in Seniors*. Toronto: Addiction Research Foundation.

Annis, H.M. (1982). *Inventory of Drinking Situations (IDS-100)*. Toronto: Addiction Research Foundation.

Baron, J., & Carver, V. (1997). Substance abuse and older clients. In S. Harrison & V. Carver (Eds.), *Alcohol and Drug Problems: A Practical Guide for Counsellors* (2nd ed.). Toronto: Addiction Research Foundation.

Bergin, B., & Baron, J. (1992). *LESA: A Program of Lifestyle Enrichment for Senior Adults with Alcohol and other Psychoactive Drug Problems*. Ottawa: Centretown Community Health Centre.

Graham, K., Saunders, S.J., Flower, M.C., et al. (1995). *Addictions Treatment for Older Adults: Evaluation of an Innovative Client-Centred Approach*. New York: The Haworth Press.

Jacobs, M.R., & O'B. Fehr, K. (1987). *Drugs and Drug Abuse: A Reference Text* (2nd ed.). Toronto: Addiction Research Foundation.

Kahan, M. (1997). Physical effects of alcohol and other drugs. In S. Harrison & V. Carver (Eds.), *Alcohol and Drug Problems: A Practical Guide for Counsellors* (2nd ed.). Toronto: Addiction Research Foundation.

Prochaska, J.O., Norcross, J.C., & DiClemente, C.C. (1994). *Changing for Good*. New York: William Morrow.

Reeves, J. (1961). *Fables from Aesop Retold by James Reeves*. London: Blackie of London and Glasgow.

West, P., & Graham, K. (1997). *Participatory research on innovative addictions treatment for older adults: Clients of the LESA program describe what makes a difference*. Unpublished report for the Addiction Research Foundation, Toronto.

www.ingramcontent.com/pod-product-compliance
Lightning Source LLC
Chambersburg PA
CBHW081156270326
41930CB00014B/3175